GURKHA
WAR POEMS

GURKHA
WAR POEMS

MIJASH TEMBE
APJASE KANCHHA
KANGMANG NARESH RAI

All poems are translated by Mr Jayant Sharma

authorHOUSE®

AuthorHouse™ UK Ltd.
1663 Liberty Drive
Bloomington, IN 47403 USA
www.authorhouse.co.uk
Phone: 0800.197.4150

Published by AuthorHouse   10/24/2013

ISBN: 978-1-4918-8094-4 (sc)
ISBN: 978-1-4918-8095-1 (e)

TABLE OF CONTENTS

WAR IS LIKE TEARS

Wiping off the stream of tears
Flowing incessantly from her eyes
I pick up my baggage with heavy heart
Heaving a loud sigh of grief-
She throws her hands tightly around my waist!

There are still hours for dawn to begin
My son—deep in his sleep
Moths are huddling around the lamp
Colliding over the same lamp
Some are spreading their legs injured
While others are already dead!

Few drops of her tears
Trickle over my boot
And shimmer at the brightness of light
I close my eyes
And, open them in a while
To look at the boots
The teardrops flowing from the boot
Had vanished somewhere into the carpet
I think—
The life of we soldiers
Is like tears!

'Please do not go to the war
Let us go back to our own country'
'Don't say that, my dear!
I have promised the Union Jack—two times
How would I say—
I am not going to Afghanistan?
It's my duty to go to war'
Unknowingly slips my arrogance!

I think—of my old parents
I see—my sleeping child
My dear wife shed into tears
Uff!
How would my heart allow me
To go to the war at this time?

There is a heap of dead moths
Over the carpet

I start hearing
Soundless music
Pouring incessant river from the eyes
And, putting garland of flowers around my neck
With her shivering hands,
She says—
'Return from the war
Like the way you are going today.'

I feel—
There are many things to say
But words don't come out
Getting speechless
I step out of my quarter
And, slam loudly
The door of farewell!

—Kangmang Naresh Rai

BEFORE GOING TO THE WAR

Once again I think—
Of myself and of my dear ones
Of things that are my own
And that I made my own
I recollect
I count
I speculate
The Reason-
I might not return
Once I set off
And if my body doesn't return
Who is to be met with?
With whom is to be talked, laughed or cried?
What is to be claimed as your own?

I might have got to repay something
Or I might have something to receive
I recollect—
The debts
The loans
The things I have lent
After I go, all these things will also go strayed.
The Reason—
I might kick the bucket
Once the person goes off
Who will repay the loans?
How will one pay the debts?
What bonds and proofs will then remain?

I might have hurt many
Or might also have pleased some
How many foes I have made?
How many friends I have earned?
I once again remember everyone.
The Reason—
I might never wake up again
Once the body goes to sleep forever
What is there in enmity?
Whom should I scare off?
Or with what should I be scared of?

I recollect—
The war at Nalapani[1]
The World War I
The World War II
The Falkland and Borneo War
The war at Kosovo
Afghanistan . . . nistan . . . istan . . . tan.. an . . .
I get pulled in those wars.
Like my colleagues—
I might also fall down somewhere in the war
The Reason—
If I win the war, I am brave somehow
But if I fall down, I will still be regarded a brave

---

[1] the first war between Nepal and Britain.

Before going to the war
One by one, I think—
Of myself and of my dear ones
Of lenders and borrowers
Of foes and friends
And,
All those daring wars of history
The Reason—
I myself can be a history
And once I become a history
I become nothing more than a mere history.

—Mijas Tembe

SOLDIERS, WAR AND MY QUESTION

On the very night of departure
Making door the borderline
I and You were standing
Inside and outside of the door.

Carrying unexpressed tears all over eyes
Carrying dormant volcano all over heart
Love on the right side of the chest
And responsibility clipped on the left
You bid adieu
To your partner dearer than your life
To that shadow lovelier than your life

To crack war against the enemies
You made your way to battlefield

No sooner you left for the war
Another war has germinated inside me
It's war-
Of your memories
Of your affection
Of your whereabouts

Swirling a Tsunami of doubt on my mind
I am ruminating of you and the war
I am thinking of my *destiny* and the frontier

Will you ever return from the war all right?
Or losing some body parts,
You will return with medals on chest
Of the wounds of bravery.

And again, I contemplate-
Can war understand the language of love?
Can war hear the call of heart and the value of tears?

I am a spouse of a brave soldier
I am a daughter of a brave soldier
I am a mother of a brave soldier
I am proud of being referred so
I take pride in this identity

And along with it comes a question
Does victory lie in killing people like oneself?
Does war understand poetry?
Can lotus bloom from the barrel of gun?
A lotus that can be adorned with love
On the bonce of a soldier's wife, daughter and mother like me.

—Anju Anjali

ME, THE POINT MAN

When I walk through the ploughed field
When I step on the rough paths
When I jump across the ditch
When I run between the walls
When I go through the tree line . . . .
Every step that I make
has a potential explosion.

Enemy might find me first
Enemy might see me first
Enemy might judge me first
Enemy might shoot me first
Every time when they shoot
I am the first sand bag to block bullets

-Run!
-Move fast
—Slow down
—Go firm
—Halt
Every step I make
Death will always be with me.

—Mijash Tembe

BATTLEFIELD, MOTHER AND OVERWHELMED HEART

Mother,
I will return;
Please have patience:
I will surely come back one day.

This time swallowed by war
Life is of no significance, mother!
Divided on the verge between life and death.
Life is but a corpse.

Mother,
The battlefield is a fearsome place
A soldier is so entwined
With rifle, bullet and grenade;
That he cannot feel secure
Unless he has motherly love knitted firmly into his being.
Mother, I need your blessings even more,
So that death will bow at your feet in reverence.

I will claim the triumph over my own death;
From the mountains of your blessings
Will rise the victory parade of warriors.
I will be held to your bosom,
And we will find a new horizon in our relationship—mother
and son.
Mother, please have patience
Making love with the Moon, I will come back.

With me also will come
The smile of rhododendrons
To cuddle on your bosom
No sound of death will echo
In the sky of your heart.
Yes, my mother!
With me also will come the VC[2]
Playing the rhythm
On my chest like great echoes from the cliffs.
No arrogance born of victory
Will accompany my coming,
Nor will there be any fear of death,
Please believe me, Mother!
No terror will stand upon my feet,
Nor will the tornado of fear, misery, anguish and torment
Swell in your adorable bosom.

In the medal glistening on my chest,
You will find your lost happiness,
You will unknowingly get back your snatched life
Finding a gleam of the Moon shining on your forehead,
You will forget your past worn out by loneliness and boredom
And will suddenly remember
Your husband, killed in Borneo war.
In course of finding a grain of happiness at every time

Mother!
Like father like son-

---

[2]   VC:- Victoria Cross

I resemble him exactly;
Same soldier, same warrior
Mortgaging pain
In exchange for life over death
I am the Same soldier
However,
Death will not take over me so easily
Death will never step on your son's corpse.

Please have patience, my mother!
Deceiving the eyes of death
I will come back to life.

It's with your motherhood and affection
That I feel insurmountable
On this battlefield now.
With all your blessings
I feel I can overcome
All the hardships of the battlefield.

Mother!
I am just a life
And you my age.
I am an empty heart
And you my heartbeat.

I will return, my mother
Please have patience
I will surely come back one day.

—Ganesh Rai

COMPLAINT

In the twilight
The sentry post of Musa Qala[3] FOB[4]
The binoculars watching high threat of enemies
The morale of soldiers like that of setting sun
The rifle ambushing on the way like the blades of khukuri[5]
The present awaiting the enemies at the door of death
The silhouette of soldiers seen on corner of cold trench
The cool breeze of villages and towns hath not the touch here
The warm weather of wilds hath not the experience here
Only seeing the river flowing nearby in its own pace
That Musa Qala hath not the nature that of soldier

Like the rifle ripped while fighting the war
Broken are all the dreams of a soldier
Like the helmet spinning while shooting an enemy
All his dreams left are whirling
Rifles are in series breaking
The war is not yet over

From the front line of war,you can see
His rifle is fell down in that cold trench
His injured body is wearied like it could never stand again
Rifle, magazine, bullets all scattered on the floor
As if they are hinting to his remaining life
His happiness soaring high up in the fumes of bombs

---

[3]   Musa Qala FOB:- Name of village in Afghanistan.
[4]   FOB:- A Forward Operating Base is any secured forward military position, commonly a military base, that is used to support tactical operations.
[5]   The **khukuri** (alternatively spelled **khukri**) is a Nepalese knife with an inwardly curved edge, used as both a tool and as a weapon.

At times when he comes back to senses
He feels like a mourning procession following him
He feels like his rifle is encased in a coffin[6]
He feels the trauma of his bereaved family
And unknowingly splashes in his heart the memories of past
In his body, the anguishes of present bulges out
And he loses his senses thinking of future

Without having got to see his beloved's photo one last time
Without having got to listen her melodious voice
He thus has to turn into soil at war
he has to touch the way of heaven.

—Apjase Kanchha

---

[6] Coffin:- A coffin is a funerary box used in the display and containment
of dead people, either for burial or cremation.

THE ARMY NUMBER-21166057

Standing on the roots of the same tree
Leaning on the stone fork of the same tree
Had he fired bullet
Shame on him . . . that bastard . . .
Luck hath it saved, you 6057
The hot Taliban's bullet missed its target
The showers of cold spoofs went past by the ear
And got struck somewhere in his abdomen
Where stung since 200 years continuously
I can see the shadow of dead soldiers

57 is not dead, Sir!
Hardly his dead-like voice could reach the heart
A fume of explosion of bomb, shattering the walls of brain
Entered forcefully inside the tunnel of ears
The silty soil of Musa Qala[7] bumping knees in calamities
Caressed his final sound
And the hills of Kandahar[8] without a blink, watched
The helmet flicking away from his head
The rifle falling on the ground losing grip of his hand
Looking at his own blood-begrimed body
Fell by that same rifle
He who fought with death all alone till the last hour
Fell down in the wink of these eyes
From the other end of this round Earth—a flat person
Before his wings, with fright, could take the flight
Flew away he with his hobbling feet

---

[7] Musa Qala:-Name of village in Afghanistan.
[8] Kandahar or Qandahar, known in older literature as Candahar, is the second largest city in Afghanistan.

On the top of a bare tree
A crane flying, not sure whether in its dream or reality
At loss of appetite for the stale flesh of human carcass
Landing its lazy wings descended off a cliff
The old vulture drooping—whether of hunger or thirst
An injured gesticulating jenny, having recently hurt her foot
Passed by this way dragging her udders
A lunatic woman hauling her bare breasts
Just passed by covering her son's corpse with a shawl
A recently raped damsel throwing her mutilated vagina
In this valley, passed by the same way
In the graveyard of his recently abducted wife
A husband burying his ego passed by this way
And when the visuals changed again
Thrusting hunger in helmet, Pouches and Bergen
Lifting thirst from the water bottle around waist
Pressed inside his wallet, never able to see in solitary
The tarnished photo of his beloved
While embracing rifle in her memories
Came forth the young soldiers from the same way
Blowing Musa Qala in the dust of stamping boots
And soaring arrogance high in the air
Targeting the barrel of rocket launcher up above
And harshly dragging Tora Bora[9] under the cruel tyres
The fighter tankers returned the same way.

---

[9] Tora bora, known locally as Spīn Ghar, is a cave complex situated in the White Mountains of eastern Afghanistan, in the Pachir Wa Agam District of Nangarhar province.

And,Wandering around the hills and burrows of Kandahar
With wings drooping of weariness
Over the roofs of Afghani houses
Returned that old Harrier taking the same sky route.

Yes . . . hiding in this same knoll
Yes . . . with elbows dug in this same ridge
Yes . . . with knees immersed in this same land
Had he fired bullets
Shame on him . . . that bastard . . .
Luck hath it saved, you 6057
The wrong calculation of cruel bullet
Shouting cold reproaches of foul words
Went by penetrating the water bottle hung around waist
But those who couldn't take shelter inside bunkers and trenches
Where are those young soldiers?
Where are those fighter tankers?
Where are those fighter planes?
From the tattered body of handicapped soldiers
The chunks of flesh and human parts
Everything blew up in the explosion of bombs
And in no time, ants carried on their head and ran away
All the brain tissues of soldiers scattered here and there
Licking the clot of blood and flesh
Stained on the stones

Before his bones and flesh could fall down
The hyena ran away with his dreams old
We know it
When one soldier is killed
Hundreds of people also are killed
When one soldier dies
Hundreds of people also die
However,
Is war only the choiceless option of everything?
The deep gash inflicted by Basrah[10]
The tears of blood of friends
Sent by Helmand province
Like a poor father returning home
Carrying loads of loan from a shylock
Returning is he
Taking the same route
Carrying the loads of flesh of his colleagues
Wrapped in the raincoat
Refused by war and ignored by death
He is 21166057.

—Raksha Rai

---

[10]   Basrah or Basra :- name of a city in Iraq

LOVE IS A DEATH BED

Beloved,
I haven't returned in the same condition
As when I left for war.
What I have come back with
In this body alone
And all other things are dead
It is hard to act as fully alive.
That's the life of a soldier.

—Kangmang Naresh Rai

THE CRIPPLED HEART

I have returned from the war;
When my wife cried placing her head on my chest
I felt that I was not dead yet
My son's innocent face gave hope.

After winning the battle,
My heart should have been delighted;
When the war was over and I was in the camp
I should not have been afraid
But every moment,
I feel as if I am still on the battlefield;
When I close my eyes
Why do I find myself surrounded by the enemy?
Why do screams of bombs, gunpowder and IED[11] echo in my
ears?
Why does cold wind blow from the windows of my home?

When I look outside through the SUSAT[12] of my rifle,
Wounds of war ache in my body,
The shadows of war perpetually haunt my eyes,
The mutilated limbs and lost hopes burn my heart.
My spirit wanders along the battlefield of Afghanistan
Ambushing the enemy near a bleak bridge in Lashkar Gah[13]

---

[11] IED:- Improvised Explosive Device
[12] SUSAT:- Sight Unit Small Arms Trilux
[13] Lashkar Gah is a city in southern Afghanistan and the capital of
Helmand Province.

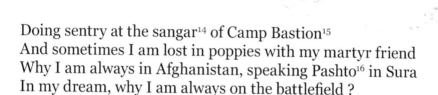

Doing sentry at the sangar[14] of Camp Bastion[15]
And sometimes I am lost in poppies with my martyr friend
Why I am always in Afghanistan, speaking Pashto[16] in Sura
In my dream, why I am always on the battlefield ?

Looking at a half withered flower,
Touching my broken rifle,
Observe !
The pictures of war under the shadow of my rifle,
The marks of tears in the lines on my cheeks,
The stains of sweat dried in my water bottles:
You will still discover the same Gurkha bravery;
You will still find the same fearless gallantry.

The doors and windows of my home question me
Where have the determinations of your rifle gone?
Where have the hopes inside your Bergan[17] have run away to?
The dreams of my wife's vermilion are still incomplete
The desires of my son, like a bud, are still unfulfilled.

—Apjase Kanchha

---

[14] A sangar is a protected sentry post, normally located around the perimeter of a base.
[15] Camp Bastion is the main British military base in Afghanistan.
[16] Pashto is one of the two official languages of Afghanistan.
[17] Bergan is a bag that is carried by the soldier.

AFGHANS

Those who are
Born with the gun fire
Grown with the gun fire
Those who
Live with the gun fire
Die with the gun fire
How come—
They are scared of it today?
Who have been living with the gun fire for generations.

Afghans !
Who inhale the smoke of the gun fire
Who drink phosphorus
Who eat grenades
Who chew bullets
Who live war
War in their kalay[18]
War in their compound
War in their home.

—No Schools-

Children !
They climb the roof top of the compound
They climb the trees
They sit on the ruined walls
They play with the dust
They run on the ploughed fields
They jump across the ditches

---

[18] Kalay:- village in Afghan Language.

Children—
They have stones and mud bricks to play with
They have leaves and branches to take with

They get toy guns, beautiful gifts, from their parents in Eed[19]
They are playing the roles—
ISAF and Taliban!

I wonder!
What will be the future of these innocent kids?
What are they going to become?
Leaders within the kids
Farmers within the kids
Professor within the kids
Scientist within the kids
Are these the future faces of Afghanistan?

I wonder
Where are the women out there?
Are they hiding inside the compound?
Are they hiding inside the Burka?
Are they hiding within themselves?
Or is the culture and the society hiding them?
I haven't seen them yet
I know, I won't see them either

---

[19] Eed:-a big festival of Muslims.

I see the elders,
Having Chaaye[20] with neighbors
Having warmth of the sun in the morning
When the red rays of the sun flash on the wrinkled forehead
of the old man
He gazes the sentry of the Sanger,
And he sips his present as he sipped his past with the Chaaye . . . .
He walks around the compound
He is waiting for his death to come . . . .
The people who can digest the war
The people who can live the war

They have walked through on the IED[21] paths
They have ploughed the mine fields
They have worked with UXOs[22]

I wonder-
How far is the peace from them?
Can anybody see it on the far horizon?

—Mijas Tembe

---

[20] Chaaye:- Tea.
[21] IED:- Improvised Explosive Device.
[22] UXO:- Unexploded ordnance.

WAR

An armed soldier am I
Blowing the siren of war.
Ready to explode
An ambush am I.
Sniffing the reek of bullets
Striding am I
In the battlefield
Putting life atop the sword.
Time marches on
Playing hide-and-seek
With bullets and gunpowder.
Awaiting the foe-men
At the garrisons
With this heartbeat dancing
In the quarry of rifle
I am celebrating
A festival of death
Barely aware of the darkness
Looming over me.

—Devendra Kheresh

THE DAY OF MY DEATH

Where did this stupid finger mess on?
Inspite of trying, why didn't the trigger get pressed?
Safety Catch was also left free
What did this forefinger get entangled with?

Victory went on his part
He pressed the trigger first
And, the bullet hit my chest open

I fell down
In a manner like
A tree standing as tall as the sky
All the lively barks and branches,
All the playful creepers of leaves
And, giving tears to youth smiling on lips
Falls down at the strike of innocent axe
Yes, I fell down in the same manner
At one shot of bullet.

Aah! I hardly found time
To yell even at my pain!
With my falling body,
Fell down also the little brightness of my impoverished hut
And suddenly extinguished
On the horizon of my heart
The faintly flickering trust inside
And woke up dreams in alarm
The mournful terror of revolt.

With my death
Also died the trust of a couple heart of my parents
Their desire of becoming loan free
Also extinguished with a single bullet in that war frontier.

I knew—
Entry into No Mans Land was a risk of life
The target of machine guns is kindled there
The mouth of mortar is faced in that direction
The enemies danger than thieves have their eyes set there
To let one experience death, a bed of ambushes is laid there.

Even then, a Gurkha soldier I
Owning every risk
In the faith of tactics and fraudulence
Tying myself with a trust
In that restricted area
Ready to celebrate an inevitable death
For sake of soldier's dignity
Unable to ward off the promises made
I was exorcising my own life
To the god of battlefield.

This hangover like the intoxication of opium
knowledge fed in brain—'Better die than be coward'
Alas! What could one do before someone's order?

Many must have thought
I went there to earn a VC[23]

---

[23]   VC:- Victoria Cross

But O my dear friends!
Don't you find any difference
Between the soldier grasped by duty
And a goat laid on for slaughter?

My timely demise in that battlefield
The red flow of blood from cliff-like chest
Has it somewhere upset her vermilion
Or has another blue river of misery stagnated?

I died
Probably the victory-hungry enemies
Must have laughed full at my death
Moreover, my village foes
Hearing the news of my death
Must have even laughed more.

Strange!
As the shameful wild laughter of my village foes echoed
The enemies who killed me couldn't laugh further.

That enemy soldier—
Brave enough to charge a bullet on my chest
Was bending on his knees—they say
And praying to his God
That the person he killed right now
May his soul get freed soon
And may he rest in heaven solemn.

—Ganesh Rai

SOUVENIR OF WAR

Now onwards the story of war
Will be a narrated one
Taking the form of dialogues
In the musings of old age.
The medals hung
On that gifted coat
Will act as the proof
Of some fairy tale characters.
And, the letters of history
Carved on his chest
Will be scored out
By the cruel boots of time.
O my dear poet sir!
Let not his gash of war wash away
By the forceful claws of your national anthem
Or by the slow poison of your patriotic verses
Let not someone peck and open his creased liver!
The children of this generation
Will play with the pages of news
They will nowadays experience
An unknown or a fantasy world
Or the stories of JK Rowling.
The war stories for them
Will be a vexing sound of music
Like the insipid winter downpour of England.
The cane is thrown once the river is forded
The footstep once treaded are lifted again for another step
The worn out boots are discarded
Similarly, the ignored face after a war
Is the soldier

And on the every poppy day
His honour is insulted and the respect he deserves is mocked.
He—a world champion of the history
Having victory over war
And after war is mentally ill
Beaten by the inferiority complex
His lame feet hit by bombs
His handicap hands gifted by bullets
His aching body inflicted by war
And amity of many wounds made in war
Sir!
He who gave up his life for the nation's life
Let not he be fed even the stale bread
He who made the nation free and prosperous
Let he be declared anti-national
He who devoted honesty and fidelity towards the country
Let he be bade farewell spoofing him of Lalbook [24]
My plead it is, sir!
He who gave a sovereign nation to you winning even the death
Let world watch the merry of his ungrateful dead body
Let he not be blessed of even a couple feet of land and a handful
of soil.

—Raksha Rai

---

[24] Lalbook:- red book, a document handed to individual Gurkha soldier
      when they retired.

THE WIFE OF A SOLDIER

Now you will rip my heart apart
And hang it
On the ground of battle
You will get lost in the reek of gunpowder
I know—
With the sharp blades of bayonet
When you fight a war of life and death
I will count those innumerable stars
Rising up above the skies
And from the window pane—left open
When I see the stars falling down at dawn
In no time, the curtain of darkness will be raised.

Who can see the wildfire
Inside my burning heart?
Who is going to believe me?
That it is harder
To live as the wife of a soldier
Fighting at the frontier
Than as the soldier himself.

I had seen you in my dreams
Your helmet was about to fall
Unable to cross the river of fire
You were searching for the fire brigade
I don't know
Whether the helmet covered your head or not.
Whether you doused the rivers of fire or not.

O my dear!
I am going restlessness
Since the day you set out for war
My heart is beating faster
Unbearable pain is screaming in my heart
As if inside me
A terrible war is going on
The burbling sound of the brook
Seems like an explosion of big cannons
As if some beautiful flowers
Are breaking into deathly laughter

As if the gush of wind
Is bringing the news of death.

Within my heart
I am experiencing
A volcanic mountain erupting
And molten lava is spilling over my dreams.

My Dear!
How can I live,
Seeing your smiling photo
Teasing your death?
But
You are bound to go to a war
I understand your duty and obligation
And therefore,
I Control the shifting hills in my broken heart.

I hope
You'll get victory in the war
Not only for country
But that victory is
Of our love
Of our life;
Surely you will make
The storm of victory
A horse of divine speed
To gallop back home quickly
And kiss gently on my cheek
Caressing my head
With your hand
You will fill the sea of love
In the vessel of my love

My Dear!
Crossing those fords of fantasies
The stars on the horizon have started falling
Most probably
After winning the war
You'll return home in haste
To cuddle in my lap
With loud hoots of victory
I am waiting for you,
Keeping alive the light of that hope
I am sure
My hopes won't prove me wrong.

—Tanka Wanem

FEAR

Under the clear sky
What are we being uppressed with?
Over the wide earth
What are we being confronted with?
Why are we struggling to breathe in the air?

I fear
I fear
I fear
I always fear . . .
Bring me back safe, once again.

—Mijash Tembe

RIFLE SOAKED IN TEARS

All of a sudden, she started falling for the rifle
Never thought of or never seen before: the hero—rifle
Suddenly, she started calling rifle her love
Suddenly, she gave her heart to rifle
Without thinking of tomorrow, she surrendered all her youth
Suddenly, she delved into dream from reality
And forgot that rifle is an organised war weapon.

Trickling tears of snow and embracing a cold hug
When rifle bade adieu for the journey of war
Suddenly, she dropped to reality from dreams
And thought—it's hard to be in love with rifle
Falling in love with rifle
Is something like staking one's courtship
Suddenly the dream—something like a reality
Suddenly the reality—something like a dream
And in no time, crossing the walls of tears
Her hero sets out for the journey of war
Stamping the boots
Following the footsteps of wounds made by rifle
She comes out in the journey of tears
Blocking the main road with love.

Suddenly her life changes
Suddenly her life changes its day and night
And everyday
In the face of the sun rising from Falkland
Sees her beloved's image.
Following the scars of rifle's memories
Reaches far across
And with the soil of his footsteps
Fills her empty vermilion
Everyday, stopping the winds coming from Kosovo
Sends the message
Of the sad hills and mountains here
Every moment, stopping the storms coming from Iraq
Flashes the news
Of the barren jungles and roads here that she walked
Holding the tremors of Afghanistan for a while
Tells the story
Of the rivers and streams here
Not singing folklores.
And, sitting on the porch of Moon
In hope of seeing the world of sun tomorrow
She reads the love letter of rifle from the battlefield
With her eyes of heart and in the brightness of tears.

—Raksha Rai

HAPPY BIRTHDAY
FROM THE BATTLEFIELD

Do not look around my son
Your dad is watching you;
I can see-
How amazingly you are climbing up
The ladder of age day by day
I can hear,
How wonderfully your baby voice
Becomesclearer and clearer day by day.
When your Mum lights the candles on the cake,
Perhaps—you can't see me there, when you blow out the candles
But I am there in the darkness, enlightening you
When you cut the cake
I am there behind you
The strength that comes out from your little arm
that's me.
My son
Never be sad for not seeing your dad
on your birthday
Dad is fighting for your country
Dad is fighting for your future
Dad is fighting so that you can celebrate
Your birthday party, peacefully.
You can understand my son
Mama told me that you are a good boy
I won't be there, because I'm on duty now
Happy birthday to you my son !

—Mijash Tembe

I AM SKELETON
THE WITNESS OF WAR

The dark clouds of war form
A beautiful war-stage of garden,
Between the bunches of bullets
When sprouts extremism
In the parade of gunpowder and bullets
Beyond the borders
The woozy fumes of artillery,
The heart-rending sound of bombs,
The dispatching stench of gunpowder,
The shrieking of innocent people,
The groaning of the injured,
The scourge of war everywhere
A humanity-raped moment
In the neighing of gun
In the reek of gunpowder
The innocent shrieks and pain of the destitutes,
Become intoxicated.

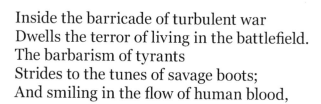

Inside the barricade of turbulent war
Dwells the terror of living in the battlefield.
The barbarism of tyrants
Strides to the tunes of savage boots;
And smiling in the flow of human blood,

That barbarism cackles at someone's death,
And Sleeps in their death-bed.
Then unable to get victory over the enemy's platoon
Wages war again—with the.
Defeaning, rippling sound:
Boom . . . Boom..
Ratatat . . . ratatat . . .
Ah . . . Oh . . .
The corpses then are scattered here and there
The ammunitions spread all over the battlefield
But under this thin membrane of barbarism
In the barren graveyards,
Many innocent soldiers are still living.

—Bimal Chamling Rai

WAR

In the long dark nights of January
The calm looking pigeons
Are hatching war silently.
Pecking meagre grains of bullets
Feed themselves with some,
And make gunpowder with the rest.
Really!
Why do these insane pigeons
Give birth to war?

The ploughmen plough
Scrape and find lives;
They Bury mines,
They see utmost devastation
Elevates summer at peak
And with stars the witnesses
They explode mortars
Really!
Why do these lunatic ploughmen
Sow wars?

In the jungles of Burma
Covering their hearts with dark clouds
Even then the soldiers
In every black night
Gather at the river bank
To collect stones for the walls of their trenches.

Having killed a few of the enemy
They return with their Bergens loaded with pain
Really!
Why do these perverted dictators
Collect wars?

On the terraces of universe
Spilling a handful measure of lava
Pleased were the stranger war gallants
But seeing the devastation at the end of war
Those who lost family weep,
While the victorious laugh.
But arrying a rifle again in their hands,
The losers become strong again
and set their hearts on another war.

Really!
Why did these bewitching stars
Teach the language of war?

In the long dark nights of January
The calm-looking pigeons
Are hatching war silently.

—Bishad

MEDAL

The aching wounds of the injured warriors
The sufferings of the bereaved family of martyrs
Why don't the people of this country feel these things?
I recollect sitting in a wheel chair

I ask the battlefield
I search in the nature of life
Where are the shadows of bravery?
Where they found in the map of this country?
The souls of those brave soldiers?

Where are the eyes of this country fixed?
Why are bold rifles of war in darkness?
Why are the brave feet helpless?
Why are the loyal chests all alone?
I ask sitting in a wheel chair.

I don't have the eyesight to enjoy the world now
I don't have the creation of restoring the amputated body parts
I hold back my tears,thinking I am a brave solider
But when my fingers touch the medals, the tears trickle
unknowingly.

—Apjase Kanchha

42

A GURKHA'S GRAVE AND POPPY

Remember the scenes from the 1st world war:
Where brave Gurkhas were fighting
Somewhere in the battlefields of Italy,
Or in the battlefields of Burma
Facing the arrogance from Hitler's army
Or the bombardments from Germany.
For the memory of brave these soldiers killed at that time,
Poppy Day is Celebrated as a tribute to them.

The land irrigated by the blood of Gurkhas
The garden adorned by their flesh and bones
The memento of the first world war
Is blooming at large over those graveyards
Flowers of love, flowers of meeting
The courage of Gurkhas
Is blossoming in every flower.

When they were alive
They had arrogant courage and pride,
But flowers don't have any such things
Time has transformed men into flowers
Time has sprouted into flowers from earth and seed
Poppies are spreading the message of peace
We are giving you a garden of colourful flowers
This garden—gifted by the first world war
Should be sniffed by every adversary
Should be seen by every extremist.

O you obstinate ears, listen to what these flowers say
Open up your eyes—that see war reeling everywhere;
These flowers letting go of the enmity,
Are sprouting up of amity.
In this garden of beauty
Let the flowers of peace always bloom.
Somewhere must be flowing such flowers of ashes
The cold teardrops of snow
But to these flowers—the witness of wars
We give a great salute of commemoration.

—Desh Subba

A FOE TO MY ENEMY I AM

I am a soldier
And a foe to my enemy
I am a person from one side
Who is working here
For the destruction of the other side.
But what can be done?
Before I turned into a soldier
I was a human being
This human inside,this human being-
Tries to be merciful and sensitive,
Desires of peace and prosperity in the world
Yes, it's the same human inside me
Trying to speak in the disguise of soldier
Trying to rebel against a soldier's duty
I try to suppress this emotion
Continuously
And make that idiot stride
    Putting Osprey
    Wearing rifles
    Carrying bullets
Holding metal detector
Make them work against the enemy
And make them a foe to the enemies.

—Mijash Tembe

ANOTHER NAME
WILL BE ADDED ON THE WALL

My Fellow!
Rifle has taken life
Off the forehead seeking blessings.

Screeching are the GPMG[25]s and SA 80 A2[26]s
Cities are Burning
Children are Wailing;
In the beautiful smiling gardens
bodies of the soldiers are falling
The glowing eyes
Of the soldiers are set on fire,
Over the bouquet of roses,
Are lines drawn in the blood.

Who says
War is unfair?
War is antagonist?
War is liberal?

---

[25] General purpose machine gun
[26] SA 80 A2 is a 5.56mm gas-operated assault rifle. It is a member of the SA80 family of assault weapons and serves the British Armed Forces as Individual Weapon.

In war,
Soldiers can be brave and cowardly at the same time
Who says—
War is guided by principles
Squashed by thoughts?
Oh my friend!
The Rifleman has stopped speaking;
The sergeant has lost both his legs,
He doesn't talk
He doesn't stand up;
His bravery and his loss will swell the pride of the Nation

And his name will be added
On the wall of the war Museum.

He is a soldier
You are a soldier
And so am I
Crushed under the feet of nationalism,
Constrained by the motherhood
Inside the meaning of these meanings,
Lies a soldier and his weapon.

—Kangmang Naresh Rai

MY LIFE

One kilo of helmet
Two kilos of combat
Four kilos of bullet
Five kilos of rifle
And, two kilos of boot
This is my life.

If I survive
Survive will my wife
Survive will my children
Survive will my friends
And, survive will all my desires
But for mere sake of survival
I will not flaunt my cowardice.

Everytime resounding in my ears
Is the rhythm of ambush and bullets
Everytime reeling before my eyes
Are the pictures of felling friends
And, everytime the memories of beloved
Keeps getting recorded in my notebook.
I shall show thou for sure
Lest I return from war.

—Devendra Kheres

ENDLESS SERIES OF WAR

Like the vast troop of army yoking in Kurukshhetra[27]
Elephants, horses and soldiers don't let hear
The whispers of sheath and sword
Nor blows anyone the conch of war
And nor does Krishna[28] arouse anyone to crack a war
Putting himself in the seat of charioteer
Like the utter silence before storm
Quiet is the modern battlefield
Once the clock of war strikes right
Fighter planes announce the attack
Canons,tanks celebrate merriment
Mortars start aiming the target
Only then the procession of soldiers
Stamping their heavy boots
Start enacting the festival of war.

Nowadays,
The scene is created
Not by the swirling of spears, swords and scimitars
But by the unfalling target of missiles
The celebration of machine guns
The outburst of grenades
The guns used by the procession of war
Fires with a continuous growling
And like the endless Nile river
Starts flowing the red river of blood.

---

[27] A mythical battlefield.
[28] Krishna is the eighth incarnation of Lord Vishnu in Hinduism.

And dreams of emperors start taking shape
Inside the dark tunnel
Starts running
The impatient train of fate orphan
Starts growing lofty
The democratic mountains
Of the despotic war leaders
And once that fume of arrogance blows
The honest soldiers in battlefield
Start beheading their enemies
The flame of conceit starts contorting over the skies
When in the world will the white flags hoist?
When is that future taking birth
Where human is never a foe to human?
Where will it end?
This aboriginal game of war leaders?
Blowing conches start that game of kill or die
Running continuously since ages
Is this endless series of war.

—Tanka Wanem

DEEP MEMORIES

Fighting in the war
We encounter crags and cliffs
We are thus living our destiny
Inside battlefield, and smell of gunpowder
Enjoying the sacrifices and extremes
In the soil of Falkland and Borneo
In the sands of Afghanistan and Iraq
We soldiers are fighting a war
Keeping hold of the dangerous and fatal stories
Creating a deep memorabilia
Of the experiences underwent in war
We are writing history from the barrel of gun.

Crossing the geographic boundary
Moving continuously are our steps
Somewhere VC[29]s and MC[30]s shine with a gentle smile
Puking black clouds
Sometimes in the jungles of Burma
Along with the shadows of thickets
We soldiers are measuring our chest
To receive immortality and martyrdom
In the scale of history
In the map of world
To conquer the world with the weapon of conscience
We are transforming into a timeless war.

—Bimal Giri

---

[29] VC:- Victoria Cross
[30] MC:- Military Cross

SOLDIER, INTIMACY AND BEAUTIFUL GUN

On the white screen of curtain
Like invisible is the current on the eyes of projector
Like the mindset of parents
Of a soldier who received martyrdom
Wailing is the gun.

Over the green roads
Like a child slitting his own testicles
With a sharp weapon
Like an old tonsured dog squealing
Licking its own breasts
Bawling is this gun.

A young soldier remembering his inamorata
Sticking on chest—the miseries of intimacy and departure
Recollecting the silhouette of husband in war
Her youth must be sobbing loneliness.

Remembering the series of incidents in life
Nowadays, I surmise
More beautiful are the guns than Miss Worlds
But very ugly are the wars.

—Kangmang Naresh Rai

WAR STORY CARVED IN ROCKS

With the bayonet of my own rifle,
I feel like stabbing my own chest,
With that bayonet, like a fiddle
I feel like slitting my own throat.
While at the battlefield,
Fighting my chest held out
Like the bunch of buki flowers,
Tied on the laces of mother's blouse
This heart racing with agitation
How I wished I could turn hard as a rock.

When I sit down on sadness
At the memorial
Built in memory of grandpa—Sergeant Bakhatbir,
Who sacrificed his life in the second world war,
When I sit down heaving a deep sigh
The war stories narrated by Hukumsingh
Reverberate in my ears.

Hukumsingh who lost one leg in war,
Who turns his crutch into his rifle
As he tells the tales of the war he fought with Japanese and
German soldiers
The letters carved on the gravestone of Bakhatbir
Start dancing before my eyes
Which reads—
"This memorial is built in the memory of the late Sergeant
Bakhatbir.
May his soul rest in peace.
Dated . . . ."

As with my grandfather's memorial,
I too must carve my name
In the pages of the brave history written by our ancestors;
I am a descendant of those brave warriors who,
Swirling their naked khukuris[31]
Amid the dusty smoke of bombs and gunpowder
Beheaded enemies and achieved victory over the world.
I will either kill or be killed,
Inspired by the adage—'Better die than be a coward'.
Caressing death on my palms,
I will stake my life,
I will march ahead with bravery;
I swear this, Mother, on this very soil!
I still remember your blessing—"May you return in the same
state as you left".

—Daya Krishna Rai

---

[31]   The kukri or khukuri is a Nepalese knife with an inwardly curved edge,
used as both a tool and as a weapon in Nepal.

SOLDIER AND WAR

The stories of the battlefield related by our ancestors,
Inspire in me a feeling of 'Better to die than be a coward'
Though wrapped in the menace of reality
I am standing—a soldier—with pride at being the son of a
warrior.

The anguish of fighting in the jungles,
The crags of the Falklands and the Frontier,
Slipping and freezing in the snow and the vicious hills
The high emotions of living, saving or dying and killing.

The sacrifice of lives in the First and the Second World Wars,
The sighs in the barren hillocks of the Falklands—
The same obligations and helplessness
To the sacrificial living history
Still continue.
A soldier—walking with a sacrificial life enmeshed in fetters
In the endless ocean of sands,
Leading a rough life on a compass-bearing
To pass the tough test of being a soldier,
To keep up the self-respect of a soldier.
This soldier is marching ahead to battle,
Suffering in the endless Iraqi sandhills
Or In the tonsured hummocks of Afghanistan
This soldier is moving ahead,
A resolute foe to the enemy whether fighting
In the midday nuclear sun, or the darkness of night,
Or in the chemical freezing coldness
Or with his worn out body being eaten by biological agents
Always the brave soldier fights on.

With curiosity aroused by the
Screens of the BBC, CNN and Al Jazeera;
When his wife, parents and relatives
Watch with half-closed eyesthe scenes
Of the battlefield
They are gazing at the experiences of life
Through the sights of a rifle.

Where corpses of soldiers lie battered
A friend just near him falls and dies
And he regards himself the unfortunate one, having to live.
The soldier, stricken with sorrow for his dead friend—
His heart of stone melts like wax, and is transformed into tears.
And, tomorrow again, the television
Spreads around the world,in the form of news,
The story of the 'Bravest of the Brave Soldiers in the World'

—Mukesh Rai

A NEW DAWN

I was aware
I was trapped in the enemy's ambush
Now that a cruel death
Would come flying and strike my chest
Boom . . . Kaboom . . .

For an instant;my mind went numb
Forgetting everyone—
My motherland/ my mother
My beloved/ my friends
In an unexpected manner—
I got drowned
In the stream of my very own blood.

And inside that enemy's ambush
I suddenly came back to my senses
I opened up my eyes
And carefully moving my battered body
Undid the cap of my water bottle and drank a gulp of life
I looked here and there—everywhere
Just to find if anyone was still there
But thinking I had given up the ghost—
All of them had already left.
And having this victory over death—
I kept waiting for a new dawn.

—Dipa Limbu Rai

THE FACE OF WAR

Fastened with the sea—buried inside the shawl of snow
The Falkland Island
Fainted by the intimidation of war
My mother's Lumbini[32] lap
Am I the war itself or
Is my desire the war?

Walking the moves of Chess board in every step
Inside the rim of obligation—mortgaging sentiments
Wearing the gleam of life on the tips of bullet
Walking I am fearless of the ambush deaths
Just to find the meaning of life.

The test of life for a soldier
Is the battlefield
Or the ugliness of war for a life
Is only the corpse.
Living death, life is immersed inside the black hole.
Bang, bang! The sound of machine guns
I listen the death's roaring laughter
Smitten into shreds this chest—infuriated
By the explosions of artillery
With the bayonet on enemy's chest
I am measuring the depth of bravery
I go blind on the extreme abominability of dead bodies
Desire I am
Living war, I am walking death, trampling life under feet

---

[32] Lumbini is a Buddhist pilgrimage site in the Rupandehi district of Nepal.

I try to find the height of life
In the red river of fresh blood
Hello, Leopoldo Faltery Sir!
I am not yet turned to stone.

Death-arrows of missiles thrown by mirage[33]
The cold sea of Bluff cove
Hundreds of souls set ablaze—period.
Ship vanishing uncovered
In the burning flames
When Belgrano ship sank
Thousands of Argentines also sank before my eyes
Under the impact of Exsoset missile
The rainbow of life lost anonymously
O war! How hard-hearted you are!
The heart collapsed breaking the walls of chest
The badly wounded corpses of innumerous people
In Gujgrin
Unable to defeat Death
The unclaimed corpses—colder than the snow
And, the red hot clots of blood
In this foreign soil of Falkland
Is looking for a handful of earth of its own land.
Atop the hills of Two Sisters
Or at the peak of Mt. Longdon
Celebrating the victory of death
This black time
A Gurkha I am

---

[33] aircraft

Dancing khukhuri[34] over the hill of Tumbledown
I am narrating Gurkha's bravery to Argentine amigos.
Life falls down—silently—defeated by death.

What type of celebration this is!
Neither day nor night—
Explodes life with bullet continuously
No traces of blue sky can be seen
The earth helpless of fear
Bombs and bullets all over
What a conference of death and life!
O Lord! How cheap is life!
However, I still choose life.

Stanley seen on the visible horizon
Like a different hamlet
Surrounded by the security of amigos
A prisoner inside their bunkers
These amigos are also human like us
However, they are enemies like us—set out
In search of death
In the lap of Tumbledown[35]
Shells of innumerous artilleries explode.

---

[34] The khukuri (alternatively spelled khukri) is a Nepalese knife with an
     inwardly curved edge, used as both a tool and as a weapon.
[35] The Battle of Mount Tumbledown was an engagement in the Falklands
     War, one of a series of battles that took place during the British advance
     towards Stanley.

This moment—
When loud voiced Harrier[36] is
Exchanging words with mirage
How I can flow along the river of emotions
With a death unaffected!
This hidden time—
Topsy-turvy inside the present battlefield
Fell by my bullet or
From an unfailing blow of a target like me
That Argentine is screaming in the bed of snow
Amigo! Amigo!
I open the eyelids of heart wide
And find that poor enemy squirming on the death-bed
I see the setting sun in the lifeless body of Amigos
The death of Amigos—must surely have
Ripped off the chest of Buenos Aires
And incessant red river of blood
Must have been flowing

On the chest of Amigo—
The motherhood must have fainted down
In the eyes-
Amigos are cursing life beating their chest
Sleeping mute is the Amigo—a corpse—on the rim of life
Sear of the rifle!

---

[36] The Harrier, informally referred to as the Jump Jet, is a family of
military jet aircraft capable of vertical/short takeoff and landing (V/
STOL) operations.

Amigo—
You are immortal at the war of Malvinas
The rest of life is still uncertain—death of life?
The mirage is still dancing in the skies
The bullets are still exploding
Amigo! Hasta La Vista!
The war is not over yet.

—Ganesh Rai

ON CURTAIN

Seen are the brave warriors
On this curtain.
Thinking of how they fell down on the battlefield
I lost my imagination.

On this curtain of eyes
How the images of those soldiers
Come dancing.
On this Earth like that of a curtain
Comes the likeness of battlefield
Performing different enactments.

In the pictures hanging
On the walls of army barracks and museums
Mud Dauber Wasp[37] are seen playing parade
And the nests built by them
The trenches burrowed by soldiers
Crawling tank on undone roads.

---

[37] Mud dauber (sometimes called "dirt dauber," "dirt digger," "dirt dobber,"
"dirt diver", or "mud wasp") is a name commonly applied to a number of
wasps from either the family Sphecidae or Crabronidae that build their
nests from mud. Mud daubers are long, slender wasps about 25-30mm
in length.

The fear of their disappearance soon
On the curtains showing our likelihood
Transformation of the crawling tank into fire
Or their falling down
The brave warriors following me in my dreams
The dropping down of pictures hung on barrack walls
Mud Dauber Wasp abandoning their nests long before
Or their sudden vanishing
What do these all signify? Whose end is coming near?

I am in dilemma
Describing the curtains of life
Sitting over the graveyard of brave warriors.

—Kangmang Naresh Rai

COFFEE SHOP TABLE

On the bank of River Avon
Stands the Victorian Cafe
Like water running in the river
Customers come and leave
Some of them revisit
And some don't
But, that cafe
Is standing firm at the same place
Where it was in the yesteryears.
The staffs of the cafe have changed
The owners have changed
But the chairs, tables and benches haven't
And, same is the taste of
Coffee
Beer
Or, whisky served there.

It's the same chair
Where Shakespeare once
Performed rehearsals for his play
It's the drink on the same table
That Churchill got influenced of
And waged a menace of war
And sitting on the same bench
Had J.K. Rowling written
The Harry Potter series
and accumulated bountiful riches.

But
Shakespeare doesn't visit there anymore
Nor does Churchill
And J.K. Rowling
Carrying loads of wealth
Has left for somewhere else

It is shortly before
When Daniel Smith and his chums
Rested on the same chair.
Under the influence of a dozen beer
Were tattling about
Bombs and Gun powders
Were narrating stories of
Afghani hills and Talibans.

But
It's just the day before
That Radios and TVs
Were broadcasting
The news of the same Daniel-
He lost life in ambush.

Hearing the news,
I am now remembering
That Daniel Smith
And the coffee shop
Those chairs,
tables
and benches

—Devendra Kheres

THE BUDDHAS INSIDE WAR

Buddha I see exactly
On the face of my fellow
Decked with different war gears
Delusion it might be
To find him as Buddha
Or it could also be the truth!

In course of patrolling
The Talibans might explode dynamites
And like the statue of Buddha in Bamiyan[38]
His body could fall down battered
Or I might also fall before him the same way
Even I may appear a Buddha to his eyes
In the soil where the grand idol of Bamiyan Buddha once collapsed
We are looking for Buddha in each other

Like the tattered idol of Buddha there
The chunks of our dismembered body
Will also be collected in our own helmets
If not the whole, some little ruins of our body
Will be placed adorned in a coffin
And we will be paid a last salutation of bravery.

---

[38]   The Buddhas of Bamiwan were two 6th century monumental statues
of standing buddha carved into the side of a cliff in the Bamwam valley
in the Hazarajat region of central Afghanistan.

Such evil and cowardice mindset will never win a war
And never is a war weighed in a scale of peace
Even then we have to win war being Buddha
And that must be the reason why
I look like Buddha
My fellow looks like Buddha
And every Soldier looks like Buddha

Had war never existed
Peace wouldn't have so much importance
Buddha wouldn't have been Buddha today
Hadn't war been there
Gurkhas would have never been Brave Gurkhas
War gave birth to Brave Gurkhas
Buddha gave birth to peace
Both took birth in the same land
In course of finding the existence of Bamiyan Buddha
We are fighting a war in the likes of Buddha
To flutter the flag of victory one day.

—Daya Krishna Rai

VC LACCHIMAN GURUNG

How I wish to offer in your coffin
A handful flower of courage
On the bosom without VC[39] medals
I want to offer a grief
I wish to leave the wounds of bravery here
To your audacity of defeating so many Japanese
I want to present a gift of memory
I wish to leave a historical fact here.

Walking are your descendants
On the roads built with your sweat and blood
But never again will the different lines of geography be killed
And never will their bosom witness the medals of bravery.

At last,
Your death has horrified our history
Your bravery and courage as sturdy as the hills
Will be seen lying carelessly
In the glass closets of Gurkha Museum.

—Bijay Hitan Magar

---

[39]   VC:- Victoria Cross

POPPY FLOWER

Last year in the war—
A Sergeant lost his life
I was bereaved by the news
And with a handful posy of flowers
I paid my condolence to him.

This time—
A Rifleman
Also didn't return from the war
My injured heart
Could do nothing more than
Offer flowers to his soul.

The coming year—
Don't know which lieutenant, captain
or army officer
Will perish in the war?
Or will get lost?
Or be injured?
Now—
I see the need of more flowers
A handful of flowers
A handful of life!

This never-ending war
This undefeatable war
Long ago
War was fought for and against
Injustice and Transgression
Rights and Freedom
For one's own existence and responsibility.

In the memory of brave warriors
Who lost their lives in war
Every year—
On the Flanders field
Poppy flowers blossomed
And with bouquet of those flowers
The brave souls were felicitated
And a call for peace was made.

But now in the Flanders field
Since a long time
The poppy flowers have stopped blooming
But the war hasn't ended yet
People haven't stopped dying and killing
With the flowers of paper
We are still celebrating
The November 11
And are sending
Thousands of brave sons
To the war
Or we are shoving them to death bed
Is the war won only by bullets?
Or will the war end only by taking lives?

—Devendra Kheres

FROM THE CAMP OF POSSIBILITY

Besides the boundaries
drawn by your memories
That blue sky
This beautiful geography
This breeze
This river
This flower
The autonomous birds
Why all of them had to divide?

In that corner of geography
Your nights terrorized by war
and, in our own courtyard
sleepless my eyes
Besides the geographical difference
Aren't same the human sentiments on whole?
Feelings don't have a fixed geography
I recall-
the evening before the Valentine's day
Dear!
Don't talk about roses here
From my skies above
drop down the red flowers of fire
And next day, as said-
Your beautiful city
wrecked is
inside the clouds of gunpowder . . .
Only left are-
Some chunks of terra ferma
drawn by your agony.

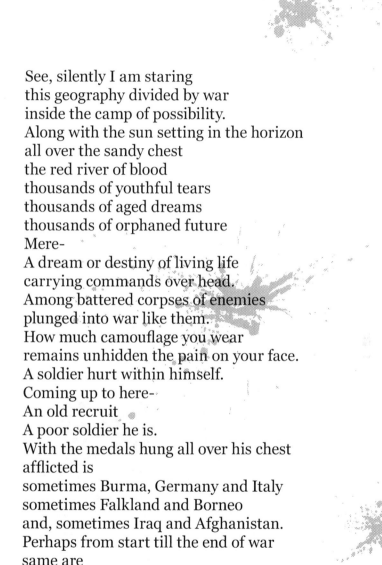

See, silently I am staring
this geography divided by war
inside the camp of possibility.
Along with the sun setting in the horizon
all over the sandy chest
the red river of blood
thousands of youthful tears
thousands of aged dreams
thousands of orphaned future
Mere-
A dream or destiny of living life
carrying commands over head.
Among battered corpses of enemies
plunged into war like them.
How much camouflage you wear
remains unhidden the pain on your face.
A soldier hurt within himself.
Coming up to here-
An old recruit
A poor soldier he is.
With the medals hung all over his chest
afflicted is
sometimes Burma, Germany and Italy
sometimes Falkland and Borneo
and, sometimes Iraq and Afghanistan.
Perhaps from start till the end of war
same are
the entire human agonies.

Okay,
Who are the annihilators then?
See, silently I am staring
this geography divided by war
inside the camp of possibility.
War giving birth to
hunger, disease, epidemic
and, finally a shoddy death.

—Laxmi Thapa Rai 'Lara'

MOON ENTRAPPED IN AMBUSH

The full-moon night is moving afar
O dear!
The quarter crescent shape of Moon
I see now like your necklace
While sitting ambush in this barren desert
Your face is dancing in my eyes
And dancing is the picture of our dear son
In the sky on a full-moon night
The moon blooming like a flower of gold
Our son used to try to pluck it and play
This moon moving towards the no-moon night
Wish I could pluck it like son
And put it around your neck

We are taming a dead peace in this ambush
In the quarter crescent dim light
When enemies will arrive the way we are awaiting
And then, breaking all the dead silence
We will start firing machine guns, rifles and grenades
The bombs-gun powders will explode like maize seeds bursting
on a roast
The stench of gunpowder will spread all over!
The reek of blood will spill all over!

And shouting loud hoots of victory
Trampling we move ahead the corpses of enemies
Whether you fight for bread or for country
In the courtyard of their beloved's heart
The moon playing brightly will be eclipsed
Neither will it pass by the edge of heart
Being her heartbeat, the cool rays of moonlight
Golden dreams exchanged for blood
Will set forever like the darkness of no-moon night
Where in fact is the rising horizon
Of the moon entrapped in ambush?

—Daya Krishna Rai

HOLOCAUST SYMPHONY
OF WAR AND DEATH

War—is death for loosers
War—is victory for winners
For that win and lose
War was, is and will always exist
Probably
For giving the same continuity
War never died
Instead rose up in jealousy
Erecting the pillar of war
Danced the wildest tempos
In the eaves of poth.

What in fact is war?
If not is the break of infatuation
Probably is a sacrifice
The history has it
That war took birth
And never died since.
The procession of wars
Jingled the sharp blade of bayonet
And beheaded people
With the barrel of gun
Walking down the human stage
Laid on by the human civilization
Though they said that war needs end
War never stopped
Instead kept growing like the skies tall

Kept flowing
The Nile river of blood
Laughing a monstrous mirth
The homicides of world wars
And beating the drums of death
Kept burning vigorously
Perhaps
That music of death will be played
For ages and ages.

Following that parade of war
I myself had attended
The mourning procession of death
Uff!
The sounds of gun
How tasteless they were!
How is holocaust symphony equal
To the spellbound folk tunes of our village?
How is excitement and merriment possible
In the extreme tragedy of someone's death?
Even then
On the forehead of history
Kindling the lamp of honesty
Enduring several wounds
Undergoing infinite pain
The mountains of woes kept escalating
The rivers of honesty kept flowing
Drawing the lines of boundary
Against someone's desire
The vast skies and earth kept expanding

Who knows!
If the hills of our own youth have collapsed
Or our own earth has foundered
Or the mourning procession is for our own death
The instruments of death
To their hearts' content
Is making music of long sins
In the courtyard of death
War must have also laughed to its content.

Had that character of war
Fell down on the battlefield
A situation where
His relatives would not have been able to
Trickle tears at his death
Obligation of not been able to offer soil
Standing by his graveyard
And not been able to wash away the sin door
Making their heart strong
With the letter delivered by a postman
Broken is a thin red thread
To endure this ill-fate
Had I been a warrior!
Great!
War spared me alone
And therefore I am reading
The reflection of my own death
On my every own face
And saying to myself—
O warrior of battlefield!

You got victory over death
Now, in the tunes of bayonet
Weaving the words of death
Play the music of war poem

—Tanka Wanem

WAR IS A WOUND

The Sarangi[40] of a folk artist
Singing the tunes of war
Isn't just crying on the streets!

In the sad tunes of Sarangi
Flowing is the river
The tears of departure.

Parents who lost their son
A widow who lost her husband
Orphans who lost the laps of their father
Cold wind of war blowing in their heart
The waterfalls cascading—the tears of pain.

What is the vision of war?
Like a blind man who lost his sight fighting
How is the brain of war?
Like the intoxicated man
Under the influence of cheap local liquor
What is the color of war?
Like the dry fields eaten up by the wildfire during draught
How is the step of war?
Like the storms and gales
What is the vision of war?
How is their body structure?
Like the earthquake

---

[40] The sarangi is a bowed, short-necked string instrument from South
Asia which originated from Gandarbha folk instruments.

War is meta pain—the pain of pains
War is meta misery—the misery of miseries
Yes, war is meta wound—the wound of wounds.
But
Why is the time fostering a war?
Why is the age living in a war?

—Jagat Nabodit

SHADOW WARRIOR

War-
A place of power demonstration
A touchstone of proving bravery
But again war-
Never you fight alone
Most probably with you
We've been fighting
A more ferocious war than yours.

While you are fighting in the battlefield
It's us who get first killed
By the enemy's ambush.
In scarcity/hunger struck heart
From the artillery you fire
It's we who get shot violently
Being the cannon shell
In the vicinity of the opponents.
And every night
Every day
It's we who get destroyed
Somewhere as 'sex-slaves'
Somewhere as 'comfort-women[41]'.

---

[41] Comfort Women were women and girls forced into a prostitution corps
created by the Empire of Japan during World War II. During the time
of war, there were millions of such women in the world.

The war
That challenges our motherhood
Again demands warriors from us only
This body
Now transforms into a factory
However,
This biological factory
Can't remain blind
Can't become feelingless
Swimming in tears
Of the tragedy with dear ones
We have to fight in the battlefield of struggle
Raped we are each and every moment,
Attacked we are only
With an intimate weapon of your war
Accepting thousand of deaths
We are obliged to wake up again
And fighting against this ugly and deformed war
We come close to you
With the misery of being neglected again
We dive into another war of life.

History there is the witness—
Series of autocratic wars
We kept fighting always
Iraq, Afghanistan

World Wars
Cold Wars
Civil Wars
Wars in every line of geography
In your battlefield,
We were merely
A sex servant, a kitchen helper
A faithful platoon of suicide bombers
And a warrior carrying guns along with you
However,
War is only your assets
Only you are the victorious.

Yes, never we were called 'brave female warriors'
Never was Victoria Cross hung on our chest
Never was an eulogy of our bravery sung
However,
Without loosing balance in all sorts of war
One who can fight continuously
One having impregnable courage
We are the real warriors-
Mere a shadow warrior you are.

—Manorama Sunuwar

GURKHA AS A STANDING STATUE!

Drrr-Drrr-Dum!
Left-Right-Left!
Standing aimlessly—is this statue
A long period of time after March Pass
This statue—instead has arrived White Hall
Standing upright for two hundred years
—it was at the same place yesterday
—it is at the same place even today
This statue—a quick march . . .
Drrr-Drrr-Dum!
Left-Right-Left!

The mourning procession is still playing parade
Thames River—trickling no tears since eons back
Hath not pain flowed there
But its parallel flowing is Saptakoshi[42]
From the bank of this time
Where has London reached
And where has Kathmandu left out?
Only Thames flows below the London Bridge
Time is thus ejaculated from Greenwich
And stands in an attention position at the feet of Big Ben
Under the midday sun
Trampling its own shadow—is standing this statue
Only around its soles

---

[42] Saptakoshi:- Name of river in Nepal

Revolves the brain of its Earth
And then his land strides but footsteps don't advance
And then his universe revolves, but pace doesn't move
Drrr-Drrr-Dum!
Left-Right-Left!

This statue-
Doesn't have hunger or thirst
Doesn't know hotness or cold
Doesn't feel sleepy or tired
Doesn't get hurt by the gunshot
Doesn't get insulted with the spitting
This statue—after arriving White Hall
Has become a real statue
The hollows in its eyes are meant for larks to lay eggs
Its head is meant for retaining pride of Gurkhas' Hat
Lungs puffed with loads in Bergen
Let the Gurkhas lope CFT[43] continuously
Fists armed with sighs
Let the Gurkhas run BFT[44] encessantly
Holding back a storm—stands this statue motionless
Blocking another Thames—stands this statue at the same place
Sigh! It's exhausted of standing on a same place
Sigh! It's fagged of resting on a same place
Unable to bend its mute limbs and squat down
This is a tree of sorrow

---

[43] CFT:- combat fitness test
[44] BFT:- basic fitness test

Germinating from its own roots, it's become a dwarf
Pressed by the Gurkha Hat from top, it's become a Bonsai[45]
A man from the village smearing camo cream all over face
Has today become a dense jungle sprouting camouflage all over
the body
Doesn't understand its own language
Doens't hear its own voice
Every night, gives voice after revelry
Drrr-Drrr-Dum!
Left-Right-Left!

Lugged inside one's own boot
Crushed under one's own Gurkha hat
Stuffed inside the sheath of khukuri[46]
With brains screwed in the lid of water bottle
And taking birth a Gurkha—from death
And in course of fighting
Making its way through the desert of conscience
And dense forest of knowledge
Fights in the battle and gets killed in wisdom
Gets slaughtered more and more in wisdom
Time and again killed in wisdom
And, in this way losing many times in wisdom
Standing is this statue here—to win something.

—Raksha Rai

---

[45] Bonsai:- kind of short tree
[46] The kukri or khukuri is a Nepalese knife with an inwardly curved edge,
used as both a tool and as a weapon in Nepal.

INJURED SOLDIER

Ask me not—
The colour of war!
The taste of bullet!
Have you the courage to hear,
Oh, journalist friend?
Better you ask—
Who got left behind in the war!
What got smashed and broken
How mines destroyed the lives of soldiers!
How suicide bombers[47] took peace

Better write if you can,
The story of a soldier
Before and after in the war
The woes of wife and children
Of the soldier killed in the war.
Ask,if you can,the injured soldiers
'Will the medals hung on chests,
Make up for the lost body parts,
And heal the pain of war?'

The soldiers who returned alive
After a six-month tour on OP Herrick[48]
March in the rememberance parade.
What would the wife of a soldier feel-
Whose husband doesn't return from the war?

---

[47] Suicide Bomber: A terrorist who blows himself up in order to kill or
injure other people.
[48] Op. Herrick:- Operation Herrick, is a code name used by British Army
during the war in Afghanistan.

How much her heart would lament!
Thinking of the words he said before going to war,
The promises he made on phone during the war.

A soldier's life is nothing more than a rifle
I am unable to surmise a life more than that.
When I got trapped in enemy ambush
At the FOB[49] of Musa Qala[50],
And I got hit by a bullet on my left wrist.
Since then I faint time and again
Oh, my journalist friend!
I can now no longer distinguish my wishes and duty
I see no difference in firing my rifle or getting fired at;
A soldier's life is nothing more than a rifle.
What I feel is-
Soldiers may not be that brave
But they are not coward either!

—Apjase Kanchha

---

[49]   FOB:- Forward Operation Base.
[50]   Musa Qala:- A village in Afghanistan.

THE WILL OF A WIDOW
IN THE COURTYARD OF WAR

Not only did they impregnate us,
But kissing our forehead
Loved us too.
Yoke to the chariot of joy and sorrow,
We ploughed the barren journey of life
And made it green
But
Nowhere they are before us
And once our buds of desire are awakened
The dream of attaining motherhood
Spreads vast like the skies
Where
The mountains of clouds stand before
The Sun and Moon seen beyond the horizon.

Carrying guns over their shoulders
And Swirling their swords
They didn't perish in the battlefield;
Instead
While running for their lives, they died
While hiding themselves, they got lost
This is not something that women are afflicted with:
With the pain of not being men.

Instead,
The continuity of nature has stopped.
Chewed by the hunger of the wars of religion;
When the faces of men have gone empty,
How is the production of our people possible
Without the drops of semen they own?
Our youth has been rendered infertile
Like formed is scum in the faces of stone
So, how are we to control
The emotions of extreme lovemaking
With the hearts of women soft as cheese

When their throats were slit by the sword of war
And
Drop by drop . . . trickled blood . . .
we were Speechless
And our eyes closed
With hopes of dousing the flames of revolt
When we looked outside on the world.
From our window
Our husbands had already perished the bucket
Leaving us behind desolate.

Why did they kill our husbands?
Who were always with us,
Smiling in our happiness, and
Crying in our sorrows.

We had heard somewhere—
That war and death
Come equally to everyone
But
This religion war is something different;
It cuts off the heads of men,
It plunges bayonets into the chests of men
And
Makes the beautiful world of women
insipid and insane.

—Tanka Wanem

AN OLD SOLDIER

It is hard to recognize his bravery medals,
Tarnished by the smoky stains of time,
The ribbons on it
Gnawed into pieces by the rodents
An old soldier gets up
To look into the cabinet
But he can hardly move;
Clutching the new cane with his old hands,
He smirks gently
Recollecting the victory over death at war.

—Kangmang Naresh Rai

ACKNOWLEDGEMENT

We would like to thank Mr Jayant Sharma, Shashi Lumumbu, Kim Brook, Mrs Sue Brook and the all the Gurkha Poets who have contributed their writings towards this book.

Mijash Tembe

Mr Tembe is a well known Nepalese poet and lyricist. He has released solo audio song's album in 2006. He has written more than half a dozen of books of different genres in Nepali language. He is also known for his new philosophical idea— Neo-consciousness (Nawachetanagraha).

Kangmang Naresh Rai

Mr Rai is one of the leading poets in Nepali diaspora. His major works include writing poetries as well as war novels. Currently, he is executive editor of the Greenwich Times Magazine in the United Kingdom.

Apjase Kanchha

Mr Kanchha is a well known Nepalese youth poet and editor. He is not only one of the activists of Nepali war literature movement but also one of the renowned haiku writers in Nepali diaspora.